"Sharon Bridgfor
the first effort of wha
novel. ...The act of the performance novel is a challenge
of exploration in forms of American storytelling. The
performance work developed over the past 20 years has
not always fulfilled satisfying experiences with language.
We are willing to now deepen our explorations of form.
Creating vocabularies and expanding dialogues centered
on diverse methods of excavating stories is the goal. How
successful we are will be defined by those of us making
the journey... This primary work [*love conjure/blues*] has
given permission to many of the rest of us to move
forward."

—Laurie Carlos, *The Austin Chronicle*, Sept. 16, 2005

"More than a novel, not entirely a stage performance,
soulful prose infused with impassioned poetry, best read
aloud or at least whispered in the mind—*love conjure/blues*
is a challenge to read, but with infinite rewards. Among
them is the essential message that, central to survival in a
black working-class world, there must be the acceptance
of love in all its varieties: 'they made poetry one syllable
at a time/they conjured themselves/love.' In telling her
story—of pretty girls and butch bulldykes, sissy boys and
strong gay men, sassy cross-dressers and assorted other
benders of gender—Bridgforth braids the spirited gusto
of gospel, the soaring notes of the spiritual, and the
bawdiness of the blues. The result is a jazzy fusion of
literary text, musical emotion, and oral storytelling,
simmering with the crushing history of a racist culture
and the defiant, quietly proud lives of Southern blacks
and queers. It's not as immediately accessible as her
previous work, *the bull-jean stories*—but it is equally
lyrical, often as funny, and much more intense an
experience."

—Richard Labonte, Book Marks column, Dec. 6, 2004

"With *love conjure/blues*, poet Sharon Bridgforth has gifted us with a soulful melody of words in the blues folk tradition. Harnessing the magic of her critically acclaimed *the bull-jean stories* (1998), she re-creates with seductive earthiness both the rural South of the twenties and thirties and the citified legacies of Bessie Smith and her queer house-party 'buffet flats.' Bridgforth's historically imagined juke joint community—populated by 'the mens the womens the both and the neither'— restores queer agency to black history in the tradition of Audre Lorde, Bruce Nugent, and James Baldwin. This poetry is not just a blues, but a sort of divine witchcraft, a stomp circle, a shout! Not jubilee, but *hallelujah*."

—Tara Lake, *Girlfriends* magazine, Feb/Mar 2005

"...That is to say, the pieces are poetic: architecture in language affording a contemplative space wherein we can lose and remember ourselves. They are metaphoric on one hand, use puns and wordplay on the other. The shared space for imagery is very inclusive of the audience—often visible—co-creative; not for or at an audience, but with. [Shakespeare, Kalidasa, Sophocles, Zeami, Jones, Carlos, Bridgforth.]"

—Erik Ehn, Dean of Writing for Performance,
California Institute of the Arts;
excerpt from "Chaos, Anarchy, Ecology,"
keynote address of 2007 Cohen New Works Festival, Austin, Texas

love conjure/blues

love conjure/blues

by
Sharon Bridgforth

RedBone Press
Washington, DC

love conjure/blues
is performance literature/a novel that is constructed
for telling.
the piece is not meant to be theatre/concert/an opera
or a staged reading
but is. the piece considers a range of possibilities of
gender expression and sexuality within
a rural/Black working class context.
love conjure/blues articulates African-American
sensibilities/history and oral traditions
for the purpose of exploring the ways that we have
survived; knowing
the middle passage/slavery/jim crow/and lynching.
the piece is a reflection of the ways that Black people
have used artistic expression—the creation
of spirituals blues and jazz specifically—to transmit
the stories of our survival/masterfully
transcending form to do so.
love conjure/blues places the fiction-form inside
an African-American voice; fitting
folktales poetry haints prophesy music and history
within a highly literary text. the text examines the blues
as a way of life/as ritual-in concert
with Ancient practices and new creations.
the past the present the future the living and the dead
co-exist together/at the same time
in a weave of dreams/Prayers/Love expressed.

love conjure/blues was developed with support from the Center for African & African American Studies at The University of Texas at Austin, where Bridgforth presented a reading of the first draft of **love conjure/blues** at a Diaspora Talk series. Bridgforth completed the final manuscript as a result of work done during a staged reading of the piece produced by the Center for African & African American Studies as part of the RACE/GENDER/NATION Expressive Culture and Representation 8th Annual Graduate Student Conference (co-sponsored by the Department of Theater and Dance and Austin Latina/o Lesbian Gay Bi-Sexual Transgender Organization).
Helga Davis – Composer/Co-director/Conductor
Sharon Bridgforth - Writer/Co-director
Featuring: Florinda Bryant, Daniel Dodd-Ellis, Marlah Fulgham,
Daniel Alexander Jones,
Joni L. Jones (Iya Omi Osun Olomo),
Sonja Perryman,
Sean Tate and Carsey Walker Jr.

The premiere of **love conjure/blues** was produced by the Center for African & African American Studies (University of Texas at Austin)
Helga Davis - Composer/Co-director/Conductor
Sharon Bridgforth – Writer/Co-director
Fred Cash Jr. - Musician
Featuring: Florinda Bryant, Daniel Dodd-Ellis, Gina Houston,
Daniel Alexander Jones,
Joni L. Jones (Iya Omi Osun Olomo),
Sonja Perryman and Sean Tate

Acknowledgments

i would not have been able to write this book without
the support encouragement and hard work of:
dr. ted gordon; dr. joni jones;
the Center for African & African American Studies
(U.T. Austin);
daniel alexander jones; helga davis;
the **love conjure/blues** cast musicians and crew;
the austin community that hosted and attended the
"soul food and salsa" house parties
(where i read early raw pieces of the manuscript);
rajasvini bhansali; ALLGO; resistencia bookstore;
bookwoman bookstore;
my loving talented sweet Spirited daughter
my mother
my First Love/Omi Osun
The River The Ocean The Ancestors The Orisha
The Buddha and All My Relations/
You have Blessed Me

THANK YOU!

and thank you
lisa c. moore for the gift of this publishing/
for the tenacity and fierceness of Vision that is
RedBone Press.

Abundance!
sharon bridgforth

"Making Holy": Love and the Novel
as Ritual Transformation
Introduction
by Joni L. Jones, Ph.D. / Iya Omi Osun Olomo

"and so now miss sunday morning and sweet t
they pray
in each others arms
in each others mouths
bodies wrapped / they make Holy
every Sabbath   love"

love conjure/blues
Sharon Bridgforth

Love as the New World Order

The most profoundly human act we can commit is to
feel. The sensation of feeling tunes us into the needs of
the planet and to the humanity around us. When the
capacity to feel manifests as love, it transforms us, frees
us from the confines of our physical selves and releases
us to the possibility of freedom.

Love, real love à la Mary J. Blige, is the most radical
move we can make. Love builds for a fertile ripe
tomorrow, a hoped-for continuation of the love and
humanity. Love connects us with the deepest mysteries of
the universe, and accessing that love is a spiritual path, a
covenant with ancestors, the divine and an unknown
tomorrow.

Such a love is indeed a transgression, because it flies
in the face of the social order that asks us to diminish
ourselves, to keep boundaries, to be dreamless for the
sake of familiarity and predictability. Societies, nations

function with an automated efficiency in the absence of improvisation, spontaneity and fluidity; without reveling in individuality and magic. In these structures, the present moment is lost in the machinery of the future, in delimiting tomorrow at the expense of the full potentiality of the here and now. The way these structures respond to the unwieldiness of their size and complexity is by encouraging uniformity and an erasure of detail.

The love that exists outside the social order is ignited in liminal spaces, those betwixt and between locations where our bounded selves can give way to something new, where the present has primacy over the future. In Alice Walker's *The Color Purple*, it's in Harpo's juke joint that Celie fully realizes her own potential for love and for joy. Here, Shug's singing captures both Mister and Celie—not only in lust, but in the space beyond the self where we have the capacity to meet divinity. It is also in a bar that the child in the film *Eve's Bayou* sees into a suspended world that her spirit is not mature enough to handle. Like a first-timer at a Black Baptist church, bombarded by the several spiritual realms that rock the space simultaneously, the child cannot process this adult world full of a hungry desire for the freedom that love promises.

The bar with all of the intoxicants of ritual—music, dancing, smoke, fire/alcohol, and the requirement of physical endurance—is a site for transformation. The people work themselves into the frenzy of spiritual ritual. The sweaty slow drags, rhythmic group slides, and bass-driven booty-shaking duets push people past fatigue into altered states. The tobacco smoke fires the nostrils and unhooks the vision, the low lights welcome spirits from other worlds, and the alcohol unleashes the imagination. Our senses combust so that we release. Dancing through the night until drunk for the Osun festival, drumming until one's hands bleed for the ancestors, singing at the sea in the dark of night with salt in one's eyes for Olokun—the sweat and pain and joy of earth-based religious ritual is the same otherworldliness of the juke joint. The bar becomes the temple and the revelers become worshippers seeking union with another and transcendence from the limitations of the everyday.

Transcendence in the bar and, I believe, in the sacred grove encourages gender freedom—a freedom unfettered by the conventional definitions of male and female. Gender freedom in which gender construction is fluid and situational allows us to live from our highest, most passionate, most engaged selves. This freedom is as much about releasing into one's self as it is about experiencing sexual union with another. Our gender is an extension of our conversation with the Holy Unknowable and cannot be mapped by external social demands. The people in *love conjure/blues* undergo varying degrees of personal excavation before finding the spiritual wisdom inherent in love. They demonstrate that male and female exist most truthfully as energies rather than bodies, and that a single body may house multiple gendered energies depending on the divine requirements of the moment. This sort of flexibility, contingency and simultaneous expression of realities challenges those with an investment in a prescriptive construction of gender. This gender freedom also disrupts the status quo's reliance on the suppression of passion, the ecstatic and the orgiastic in all of its possible forms, because to achieve gender freedom is to chase desire and transgress convention, if necessary, in doing so. In this way, *love conjure/blues* offers us alternative possibilities for masculinity, femininity and other that allows for a dense and textured experience of gender.

The Novel as Performance

Transgressing the social order requires a transgressive aesthetic, a sense of beauty and order that is as transgressive as the politics that undergird it. In Yoruba, *igede* roughly means "the realm in which words transform." This is a critical concept in the understanding of this new genre, a performance novel, as created by Sharon Bridgforth. Yoruba theologian Iyalorisha Aina Olomo explains, "*Igede* is using words to transfer, activate, and attach power. The realm of *igede* allows the spiritual initiator to use words to move and direct energy from one place to another, from one space, time, or object and attach it to another." (104) This transforming does not happen with the words set on the page; rather, igede exists in the saying, in the naming, in the embodiment of words. This concept promotes an understanding of narrative not only as embodiment but also of embodiment as the ingredient for transformation. Slave narratives, in which the blood and bone facts of slavery are blunted by the remote fixedness of print, give way to freedom shouts—the fully embodied, urgent, self-conjuring that calls into existence a new day. The body itself displays its own intellect—a precision of gesture, voice, eye gaze and stance—and in so doing taps into a spiritual realm and brings that information to the earth plane.

Fashioning the novel as performance carries the interaction of storytelling, the efficacy of a sermon and the transformative power of a Yoruba praise poem. In this genre, the novel is enactment—reading is loud and alive and participatory.

In Toni Morrison's *Sula*, throughout most of the novel the narrator exists as an omniscient observer telling the story with no sense of interaction with the reader. Then, while describing a woman and man making love, in a startling moment of exposure the narrator says, "uh huh, go on, say it"! (90) Right in the midst of all of that narrative distance, the narrator pulls the reader into the story and positions the reader as another neighbor in "The Bottom." The reader is invited into a full gossip session around Nell's betrayal and Sula's slip from reality. The reader and the narrator become active collaborators and witnesses in the world of the novel.

Likewise, *love conjure/blues* asks us to bring our voices and bodies and range of experiences to the act of reading. The novel is meant to be sounded out while read—so that the punctuation guides the feeling in the sentence, so that the bold type speaks differently than the capitalized letters, which shouts a story unlike the words that are no words at all, but spaces and sounds and feelings. So when the novel opens with

cool water
rum
beer vodka gin
liquor liquor liquor liquor milk

centered on the page with no capitals, we know that the look of the text will tell us as much as the words themselves. Is this a conjuration, a shopping list, a fragmented memory—or all of these possibilities at the same time? As readers we get to interact with this novel with a heightened attention, our senses poised for the nuances of spelling and syntax and typography.

remember
remember
remember

To tell a story is to construct a history, to assert a vision of reality. A history links the living with ancestors and divinities across spatial and temporal dimensions, moving back to retrieve lineage lessons and forward to cast a vision of what might be. The Yoruba concept *itan* speaks to this act of storytelling, and meaningfully extends beyond it. Yoruba scholar Olabiyi Yai explains the action inherent in *itan* when he writes of *pitan* which "means to produce such a discourse that could constitute the Ariadne's thread of the human historical labyrinth, history being equated with a maze or a riddle. *Pa itan* is to 'de-riddle' history, to shed light on human existence through time and space." (109) An *itan* enacts the story of a people or town, and *love conjure/blues* continues this ancient performance tradition from a decidedly contemporary vantage point. This performance novel is an *itan* of a fictional community that will be instantly real and recognizable to many readers. As with any strong *itan*, *love conjure/blues* reveals some of the mysteries of human existence by challenging traditional understandings of reading and participation, sexuality and sensuality, racial identity and ancestry, and the ritual performance that makes community. The experience of *love conjure/blues*—the convergence of spiritual worlds and the embodiment of those worlds through reading— is the act of "making Holy."

"the Peace we Pray
the poem we pen
the bridge we make
the song
that dance/is us
and we are

free
free
Free.
cause/We are
Love."

love conjure/blues
Sharon Bridgforth

Joni L. Jones, Ph.D.
Iya Omi Osun Olomo
Associate Director,
Center for African & African American Studies
Associate Professor,
Department of Theatre and Dance
University of Texas at Austin

Works Cited

Olomo, Aina. *The Core of Fire: A Path to Yoruba Spiritual Activism*. Brooklyn, NY: Athelia Henrietta Press, 2002.

Morrison, Toni. *Sula*. New York, NY: Alfred A. Knopf, Inc., 1973.

Abiodun, Rowland, Henry J. Drewal and John Pemberton III. *The Yoruba Artist*. Washington, DC: Smithsonian Institution Press, 1994.

love conjure/blues

cool water
rum
beer vodka gin
liquor liquor liquor liquor milk

honey
watermelon
candy
coconut cake cookies
rice roots peppercorn
hot hot hot

cigars pigsfeet cigars
swords flames thunder
attitude
attitude
drumming

it's a party it's a party it's a party/in my dreams
a party. flowers mirrors cowrie shells and pearls
ocean sunshine
lightning moon
wind clouds
sky
deep woods crossroads/the dead   living
it's a party.
the dice is tossed

5	7	6	9	3	4	8

again

9	4	8	6	7	5	3

again
yellow purple blue white red black green

1

again
drumming
again
drumming
again!

*   *   *

lawd/i'm gonn bring my burdens
bring my fears
bring my sorrows
bring my tears
gonn lay them down/lawd
gonn lay them down
i'm gonn lay
my burdens down...

we is peoples borned to violence. not our making and
not our choosing. just the world we came to. fighting
like animals leashed in a pen. maimed if we don't
win. killed if we don't fight. so we been
perfecting/fighting to win
the whole of our time here. and though violence is
not our first nature   sometimes
violence boils the blood/explodes in the veins.
sometimes violence
shows up unexpected
and just claims a nigga.

see/what had happened was
one night bitty fon
walked up on nigga red/over to king creole's catfish
cafe.

parently

nigga red's woman
peachy soonyay
been tipping around with bitty for years. and
nobody
had a clue. fact is/it wasn't the kind of thought most
likely to cross a mind
as it was not an understood possibility
or yearned for idea
        well/maybe some folk had the yearning
        but
anyway

see/bitty and peachy both what you call long nail girls.
each one primp and fuss over they hair outfits and
lipstick nails and shoes shape and such and all and
well/we thinking them two fluffing up for a trouser
wo'mn or a man or
both/but nobody figure they been giving   attention
to one the other.
after all
how
on earth
could two primpers
work out all the mirror timing necessary to start the day.
well/i guess they proved our minds was real small not
real smart at all.

anyway

what we did understand was that nigga red had done
whooped on chased down and squished peachy so
many times in so many different conflictions/till we
each done carried a bruise from pulling peachy from it.
till finally/on this night
it had just got to be all too much. anger raised up

3

sharon bridgforth

claimed bitty
poisoned she mind
sent her stomping down the road
put a stop to peachy's been-beat days.

na/bitty
a big wo'mn.
got she name not from the size of her body
but from the small of them dresses she wear.
that gal could pack more into a teeninecy piece of cloth
than a fool filling up in a jook jernt. and always wear
red.
wear it like a tree wear bark.
look real good too.
black/like night glazed in chocolate. tall as any man
and just as thick/legs long enough
to wrap around you two times/each thigh big as it want
to be/she got
enough curves to spin a train off the track/and enough
behind to stack your plate on.
bitty wear them little pieces of red/with her two thick
braids always hanging
just
over she titties.
chile
the experience of looking at bitty
could be weaponous.
kill you if you stare too hard. so much a pleasure.
ha!
anyway
and see/what had happened was

it was the seventh hour before sunrise.
bitty stepped into king creole's. with the light of night
following her

4

past the front counter/quick she like a dancer trying to
get center with a good song/quick she turn on the high
of her heels moving/quick she keeping perfect time
inside that fateful moment/bitty walked quick in a
straight line through the crowded room/past the barrel
deep with crawdads/past the booth piled high with
shrimps/past the table filled with catfish/past all us
paused in the pleasure of she red/bitty moved quick
through the jernt
then suddenly
she stepped/dipped down/swirled around/shook out
she shooter/circled/reached and laid nigga red slump
in her chair   pow pow pow
then bitty did a little shimmy place back she
shooter/and
turned out.
by the time we got a hold to the fact that
happy time
was over
bitty was outside leaning on the side door
lighting she pipe.
by then
mannish mary start to wailing   naw!naw!naw!
snotting and carrying on till she pass out.
          we understand she burden for bitty.
          see/mannish mary been in love with bitty
          since they was cotton pickers/too small to see
          over the row.
          but mannish mary carried them feelings in
          silence/all the years
          like it too fragile to speak of
          too sacred to look at
          or touch.
but we all knew.
so we just went on/carried mannish mary stretched out

5

next to nigga red.

na
wasn't nobody
upset cause nigga red shot down.
hell/that sapsucker too hateful to die
she over to reverend honré's right na
talking about how she done found Jesus.

umph.

well
anyway
bitty was peachy's knight in shining heels that night!

but na
bitty in jail   which don't hardly seem right.
cause/bitty was out to protect peachy from nigga
red/who we all know'd would have whooped peachy
from here to her Maker had she got home and found
peachy packed
and sitting over to bitty's house/perched for a new
day/which is just where we found peachy come time to
tell bout bitty in jail.

what bitty done
was in act of self-defense   for peachy.
na/sheriff townswater
understand this.
but the law don't/so we got to find a way to make the
law bend for the facts of it.
and we will.
meantime
the law got our sweet bitty in jail.

but chile
bitty/making do.
she know we gonn get her out
so she catching up on dreaming and rest.
gots her mirror
and combs and things. and she peachy come by
every day
bring meals
a spray of perfume
and a kiss.
so we all proceed as usual
till time to raise up on the law.

give me a little bit of bitty
cause a lot's too much to take
say/give me a little bit of bitty
cause a lot's too much to take.
i'll handle what i can na
you can serve me the rest at my wake.

slim figurman
handed a stranger a card what read
figure's flavors.   the world's finest.
come get a taste.
slim like to press them
handwrit cards
to folk coming through for the first time.
he be all dressed lik a fancymann
talking so many circles/till don't nobody know what
the hell
he talking about.
the new to it/always stand for it
nodd here and there

throw in a word when slim take a breath.
probably is all slim really want after all
somebody to listen
talk for a bit.

anyway

we all know
slim call himself running a ho house
but slim ain't running nothing or nobody.
so the place he call figure's flavors/we calls it
bettye's.
yessuh/cause slim's sister bettye be the one running
that jernt.
and what it is is the best blues inn in the country.
first off bettye know how to keep a clean room
so the stopovers always be happy/feel rested and cared
for
but more important/bettye can cook so gotdamngood
make you want to kick your own ass. i trying to watch
see if bettye been throwed some powders off in them
pots/make
the cooking so much excitement
for the tastes.

anyway

chile/musicians from states away haul they music over
to bettye's just
to be up in there   get some. don't even charge bettye
to play/course na
some of them tasting more than good cooking from
bettye.
look like her favorites   be extra fed. but they all of
them gets tips meals and a room/long as they willing to

work/and play hard.

and do the jernt be packed!
mens womens some that is both some that is neither/be
rolling all up and between the sounds/laying up in
them rent rooms/and dancing off all bettye's home
cooking.

anyway

it was a hot night after a hot day.
the peoples was in they finest/fresh pressed and set for
whatever bettye's was about to bring. it was rib night
the start of the weekend. folk was still   eyes bright
hearts light pockets packed full of laughter/and on the
ready.
that night was a wo'mn named big bill what rose up out
of bettye's room.
big bill had on the finest suit i have seen to this day.
come in with she suit black/hat low/glasses dark/and
shoes so shining make your head hurt. big bill walk
through
the crowd part/as she make way to the piano in the
corner of the room.
big bill's long legs reach strong
one powerful in front the other/her unbuttoned jacket
open close open close
as she walk/pants pull here here
here
material ripple across she crotch   which appear
packing a large and heavy surprise   i glance over to
bettye/see she seeing too/smiling down where big bill
pants pull and ripple large/and not so subtle in the
crotch. bettye fanning
still   sweat run all around her face.

i ain't got time be looking at bettye/look back
big bill taking she jacket off/take she hat off/slowly roll
up one crisp sleeve/then the other/loosen she tie/turn
her big broad back to the room/sit down/and ever so
slightly nodd she nappy head. at that guitar sam pull
up take a chair next to she. big bill nodd again even
more slight/and a big ole powerful sample of wo'mness
stroll center the room. sway step smile sway step smile
sway sway she went till she in place standing center
inside a moment of stillness. then suddenly/the three
of them hit a note
all at the same time/*aaaaaaawwwwwwhhhhhh*
went the sound   and i declare some kind of hunger-
spirit swept through the room.
took everybody's mind in one swoop.
after that
wasn't nothing but bodies feeding the feeling till
sunday sunrise just before first service. shiiit. we still
rest-broken from all that business.
big mama sway/singing

> *i gots geechee lips*
> *i gots geechee hips*
> *i gots a geechee kiss*
> *that you'll never forget*
> *but you got to*
> *show me that you want it*
> *show me that you need/so*
> *if you can't show me that you want it*
> *go on/pack your thangs and go.*

chile
what a time.

something about they sound almost stop my heart.

i knew it weren't the liquor
        cause wasn't nothing in my cup but that
        strong-ass coffee bettye serve/which could been
        overwork my heart/but i don't think so.
see/bettye don't allow no drinking in she jernt.
not since she lost her first love lushy boudreaux to the
guzzle.
naw/lushy ain't dead
thats her yonder holding up the back of the jernt.
bettye lost lushy from she bed   when she kicked that
drunk ass out one last time.
been upset about that ever since. mostly at herself/say
she got so caught up loving what lushy could have
been/she wouldn't see what lushy really was.

anyway

lushy don't drink no more/ bettye don't like the smell
of the drink/reminding her of the hard times/so we all
forced stay in our right minds when we come to bettye's
        well not all of us/cause you know any fool can
        find a way to tilt they cup if they want to. but
        bettye's no liquor rule do cut down on the free
        flowingness of it
which is a relief really
because usually with the drinking come the looking and
the looking bring the knives/cause folk can't just look at
they own peoples they gots to always cast a looking at
somebody's somebody else/and the knives bring the
cussing and the cussing bring the swoll chest and the
swoll chest
always
interrupt the good time.

but the good time don't hardly get stopped at bettye's

11

so i been happy as a greedy cat in a rat shack.
yessuh / i been happy / yeah.

aaawwwhhh   aaawwwhhhaaawwwhhh
aaawwwhhh   aaawwwhhhaaawwwhhh
aaawwwhhh   aaawwwhhhaaawwwhhh
aaawwwhhh   aaawwwhhhaaawwwhhh

dey used ta hang niggas by dey thumbs
aaawwwhhh yessuh if'n a nigga had da
nerve ta tink dey life wuz worf mo den a
dog or cat dey'd strang dat nigga up.
aaawwwhhh. yessuh dey tookn my own
daddy data way saw dey take he my own
daddy dey kilt he cause he a smart man too
smart to be able to hide it so dey took he
cause he weren't able to mask him
brightness and aaawwwhhh yessuh

my life it ain't never been de same since
dat day i saw dey stringed

my daddy i saw he hanging from de tree by
he thumbs.

aaawwwhhhh when certain kinda things
happen sometimes you jes aaawwwhhhh

thats my gran-gran-daddy/big paw/my father's
father. every day they say he tell that story at
sunrise/he tell it like he praying/like he not really in
the room/like somebody else speaking it for him. they
say each morning when he tell it/it's as if you just

happen to walk into a conversation he having   cept
ain't nobody there but him.

**this is home. the place that earthed you. it's a sore/a
wound/this ground/the place i grew up in.**

thats uncle daddy/he my father's father. i think he
done heard big paw's story once too many times/is
now a little touched by it
or something.

i am the cry that won't come out i am the pain stuck i
am the me that never was sorry now i am for the
moments i choked away for the lost touches diminished
faded like yellow against the sun.
i was born too early to be allowed to exist i was
drowned the day i was born of heartache and loss i am

that's big paw's sister ma-dear. they all lives here/big
paw uncle daddy and ma-dear live here at the home
house with my mama the wife of my daddy/who dead
for some time now. one day my mama called me in
the city/said **chile come home/the ole folk want you**.
not knowing what that mean/but being used to doing
what mama say/i got quick down to the home house.
there i found mama standing on the porch with she
bag packed. she said **bye gurl   i be back**. i
thought/well i guess/mama need a time off from the
home house big paw uncle daddy and ma-dear. **bye
mama** i said/from the porch waving waving waving till
she disappear in the road.

i turn to go in the house and there they were big paw
uncle daddy and ma-dear/standing around me   justa
staring/smiling big ole toothless love. i hug them each

tight tight. go in the house unpack in mama's little room/what used to be her and daddy's.

we peoples got made in de way south. i hab been made new papers ova and ova forta git em prayers jes right/lay em prayers south of de water and dirt/jes under de light of de candle. na. what i needn be a real shoutn so dat we bringn plenty wittness from de way south place to guide'n de babies safe home.

tell only God and the preacher yo prayers write what you wish on parchment paper/then hide it from yourself for one year. go back to it/and know the power of God.

with broken teeth and bodies that have gone unchecked for years
we've been living here through careless times and danger

gurl you better listen good. we telling you something/you hear.

big paw uncle daddy and ma-dear started talking to me. problem is they talking to me in my dreams. in wake time/they just smile they big toothless smiles hold my hands/taking turns for long walks in the evening/work the garden early morning/clean house mid-day. they be sweeping/brushing the floor with flower water and powder every morning early i wake to one of them staring down at me smiling smiling. till finally i don't know what day it is no more and i can't separate my thoughts from words words from dreams dreams from prayers said out loud/and lately i'm

14

thinking i'm visiting them in they dreams too.

is you done emptied de water from under de bed/shredded da paper/dumped de dirt/blow'd out de candle/make room for de new dream'n? yes i have done all that/and i cleaned with smoke and powder/placed my prayers on parchment paper surrounded by water/hidden **good. now set the candles in the east window/circle earth around the bed and**
gaga gaga gaga/ga   gaga gaga gaga/ga   gaga gaga gaga/ga
here they come now

i am he that was king/captured sold and shipped for selling *i am she whose tongue they took so as not to tell* i am he made to walk chained next to a wagon cross state lines *i am she who lived in the woods/leader of the ones that fought* i am he that scouted getaway time *i am the seer in the night* i am the runner through the corn *i am the seer in the night* **i am the crawler in the light** i am the one that got away i am elizabeth daughter of cora the child of sarah **i am the one that holds your prayers**

shuffle fast clap'n circle smoke praise moan'n shuffle shout'n shuffle fast sing'n shuffle dance'n shuffle fly holla prayers home circle smoke shuffle praise
we been learned to dream cause in wake we had to be dead.
you is free cause we was captive
you are the one we been waiting for
gaga gaga gaga/ga   gaga gaga gaga/ga   gaga gaga gaga/ga
wake now!

aaawwwbhh aaawwwbhhhaaawwwbhh
gagaga gagaga/*aaawwwbhh aaawwwbhhhaaawwwbhh*
gagaga gagaga/*aaawwwbhh aaawwwbhhhaaawwwbhh*
take me now lawd

15

aaawwwhhh aaawwwhhhaaawwwhhh
straight up to Heaven
aaawwwhhh aaawwwhhhaaawwwhhh
don't leave me here
aaawwwhhh aaawwwhhhaaawwwhhh
i need a Saving
aaawwwhhh aaawwwhhhaaawwwhhh
take me now/lawd
aaawwwhhh aaawwwhhhaaawwwhhh
take me now
aaawwwhhh aaawwwhhh aaawwwhhh
take me now
aaawwwhhh aaawwwhhh aaawwwhhh
take me now

big bill gave bettye her story like it was a fresh flower
like she handing herself cut open/for the first time.
bettye patient as the day is long   kind of.
so she just sit with she coffee
stare off the porch till big bill ready to tell it.

back home
ain't nothing like here
naw
Colored blood still feed the soil there.
to this day
the smell of it/that
smell of death festering/still haunts my dreams
keeps bad memories wake.

back home
folk spend all sunday
in church/wailing rolling shouting to Jesus/trying to lift they
burdens.
daddy say Jesus need a lifting fridays and saturdays to be

*ready for the load of sunday. daddy say thats why he play
his guitar so hard   say he playing for Jesus
trying to lift ole Jesus up.*

*i got seven brothers and three sisters.
but i was the one daddy handed a guitar to/he say before i
was born
he dreamt the blues in me. mama say thats nonsense henry
b. just go on and say it/that child is your favorite! but daddy
wouldn't never single out one/hurt the rest of his children
with words like that/even if it were true. besides daddy
loved all his children with all his heart/and he made sure
each one knew it.
mama knew it too she just like to stir.*

*life was bitter sweet back home.
we had our very own house. it was small but well put
together/mighty clean and full of the best cooking this
county have ever known. daddy's daddy sharcropped his
entire life to buy that little house/on that little old plot. it
don't seem right that he had to pay for it/all them years of
sharecropping
and the fact that it was the White stonewall's that had
enslaved him and all his people that he had to pay for that
little ole piece of property. but he did
and he was so proud.
but soon as granddaddy stonwell got that deed
well
he passed that night in his sleep. look like he smiling
soft/resting so sweet through the night holding that deed in
his hand. he never woke up/but he went to Heaven holding
on to promise for his family. so me my daddy his daddy
and all of us come up right there on that land. only acres
away from the White slave owning confederate flag waving
woman violating klan joining stonewalls.*

17

yeah. well.

i ain't hardly going back there.

sometimes things do come back to me/make me smile.
like i remember folk used to drop by our house every friday
night for momma's fish fry and every saturday for daddy's
okra stew. daddy made extra coins playing his guitar
back of the house on them nights. after the cooking the
eating the laughing the laying back daddy pick that guitar
till the people couldn't take no more.
then he'd get down the road with it/to all the little jook
jernts and backyard shacks he could walk to. i declare/the
guitar ain't never been played better
than when ole henry b. stonwell got a hold to it.

far back as i can remember daddy had me at his side while
he picked that guitar.
once i got old enough/he took me   walk them roads to play.
i believe he wanted to show me how to make my life work.
daddy say too many a good song done died in the heart of a
fool. don't drink. don't waste your money gambling. groom
hard. remember your manners. and always/take care of your
guitar. that guitar is grandchile of the instrument that our
African/pappy passed down to us. it got the power to reach
Jesus.
once Jesus hear you He'll send you down a new song for the
old.
make everything alright.
yeah. well. and daddy was a fine example of what he
taught too.
unlike most the church folk who be filling our yard fridays
and saturdays dancing to daddy's guitar hard as they be
dancing in the church aisles on sunday/cept sunday through

thursday they act like we sinners and they saints.
daddy say folk liable to act that kind of way when they
trying to get a release from they burdens. well/and you
know ain't no better release than from a right-picked guitar.
i come up playing the guitar just like my daddy taught me.
it's my church   same wail same shouting same rolling
same Holy Ghost
with a little extra.

life go quick back home.
if the White folk don't get you/picking cotton will
or the stump liquor a backyard fight or
your own heart.
thats what carried my dear sweet daddy to Jesus
his own heart.
the doctor say it just stopped.
too many years of too much.
maybe sweet Jesus just wanted a friend to sit with
help send down the songs.
i have missed my daddy every minute of every day since
that one.
every night i pick my guitar up/and Pray to daddy/who
sitting with Jesus.
i give them both the glory
every night.

the last thing daddy said to me was you ready now baby.
move on/get out of this here place. before it kills you too.
i caught my daddy's last breath.
i closed his eyes.
i hugged my crying mama
each brother and sister.
i picked up my daddy's guitar/asked mama to bury mine in
the ground with him.
and i left.

i never been back.

i done kept moving/up and down and all across
the road/in and out of every backyard shack and jook jernt
from backaway to backaway. i ain't never had a drink. i
don't gamble. i am always hard groomed.
i keep my daddy's guitar best kept.
and daddy and Jesus been touching me with a new song
every night.

thing about it
i never believed that anyone would ever in this life love me
as much as my daddy did.
i guess i never wanted to love no one that much back/chance
so great a loss again.
so i never gave much to love. i just take a little give a little
and move on.
return back to it sometimes/then leave again.
i done moved in and out of love quicker than is possible to
explain.
saved all my heart for this here guitar.
till now.

what i am telling you bettye
is that i love you.

i want you to have my heart.
i want to send my songs to you now woman.
daddy with Jesus   they alright.
i know i'll be alright too
if you'll just take my hand
and give me your heart in return.

dance with me mama
come on dance with me all night long
say/dance with me mama
come on dance with me all night long
you bring the rhythm baby
and i'll carry you/the song.

what it was will never be again/not
nothing like it
ever   it was

after midnight/a cup of cobbler and two smokes late
a woman in a red cut dress slit near up the ass
swayed to the center with colorcolorcolors wrapping
she head and
dipped V framed breasts/peeking packed tight
she standing there swaying side to side moving to the
piano/side to side till all the feelings in the room lift
the woman singing

> *weather man don't know*
> *how hot it is in here*
> *oh no/he don't know*
> *just how hot it is*
>
> *says its ten below*
> *knee deep in snow*
> *but oh no i'm so hot*
> *in here*

it was the sound of heat/perfectly pitched.
heat so clear you could see yourself/past
the seem-to-be laughter the thickened memories

21

past the backaway moon/your own heartbeat/past all
the asses rocking/the
packed tight woman carried you in her voice
so deep between her notes till
wasn't nothing to do but stretch out in her sound
and cry
about everything there ever was
cry
about all the nothing
cry was all there was
left to do was
cry.

it was magic
when that woman stepped up
everybody fell in love.
it was a magnificent juju/sweet as it gets.

he talking about big mama sway
yessuh/big mama sway always could work a sweet
juju.
she make mystery clear
when she sing
holla/unrumble the earth/cloak with the colors of her
soul.
thats why big mama sway wear her head wrap loud as
thunder
so as not to be messed with/when she step stroll step
she big ole tasty self
step stroll step she roll the crowd like dough/when big
mama sway get front center all business known and
not
bout to be taken care of.

bring your burdens
bring your fears
bring your sorrow
bring your tears
lay them down/down on me

won't mend your mess
wont' fight your fight
ain't gone fix nothing
or tell you everything's alright

but i'll be that place mama
you can come and just be
so come on baby
bring your burdens down on me

she get the peoples so full of one the other till
don't nobody know what really going on.
but i do
ummhumm/i see what it really is right there/is she
ain't singing
na/suh she doing a work for big bill
ummhumm
from big bill straight to bettye
by way of big mama sway.

na first how i know is
big bill sitting at the piano
piano ain't big bill's main thing
she a guitar man.
second
big bill got she face low under she hat
all to the wall giving her back to the people
that
so she can put all she mind on what she doing

ummhumm/i been around
too tired na to get full of anything but the truth
and what the truth is is
big bill
trying to tie up with bettye
so big mama sway swirl big bill's heart all through the
room
cause thats just how they working that thing
ummhumm/sho nuff indeed!

what i don't know is how bettye gonn take to it. cause
everybody know
lushy use-to-be drunk ass done just
ruined
bettye from sweetness.
and that is why big mama sway step in for she
friend/singing

> *i'm going home now baby*
> *i'm going home with you*
> *say/i'm going home now baby*
> *i'm going home with you*
> *you are my woman*
> *and baby you know i'm your woman too.*

big mama sway sang so hard make the Holy Ghost
wake up
swoosh all up through the jernt. folk get to
sweating/shouting dancing till
sho nuff
they saying
sweet lawd
they holla
thank you Jesus
they shouting

and big mama sway just keep at it
> *take me baby*

ummhumm/**they saying**
> *i want you to take me baby*

i know it/**they rolling**
> *take me make me yours*

yes sir/**they dipping**
> *take me baby*

here here/**they singing**
> *take me make me yours*

i declare/**some fall out**
> *take my hand now wo'mn*
> *take my hand forever my dear*
> *say/take my hand now wo'mn*
> *take my hand forever my dear*
> *i pledge my love to you always*
> *won't you pledge your love to me too*

there ain't no turning back
na

after lushy
bettye's heart had done growed callused
and scarred. opened too wide one too many times
pulled apart
cut to shreds.
feeling not young or hopeful
bettye shut her bloody heart/closed it for good.
and wasn't nothing
not no juju no song no smile
no sway could cause bettye open/chance it rupture
again
not even big bill

unless that is
big bill were to give bettye her heart/open first   wide
and raw and
completely.
but big bill didn't live in her heart/not really
so she did not posses the key to giving it away.
so the two of them laughed and played layed and loved
dreamt and waited
holding each other/from far away
safely
and
unopen
wanting wishing for more they
sang and danced to the saddness of it all.

*green and red/purple and orange/yellow and
blue/with Light
stir and simmer/smell and smile
dance pray smudge
drum
remember.
green and red/purple and orange/yellow and
blue/with Light stir and simmer/smell and smile dance
pray smudge drum remember. green and red/purple and
orange/yellow and blue/with Light stir and simmer/smell
and smile dance pray smudge drum
remember...*

**the Houma   the swamp the woods yonder
the Fon the Ibo the Yoruba the Wolof/tied lashed
lashed/opened
still fight.**

the Houma with Tunica Choctaw Chickasaw
here before the before
know night and moon hear trees and earth
drumming drumming
hold on
drumming drumming
on the way
drumming drumming
the Houma the swamp the woods yonder the moon
they signal with drum
untie the Fon the Ibo the Yoruba the Wolof
clean swab wrap quick here here here
up swamp through woods past yonder fly
not seen.
the Houma the Fon the Ibo the Yoruba the Wolof
free
free more.

sun spoon moon make rain
the Houma the Fon the Ibo the Yoruba the Wolof
the swamp the woods yonder the moon they signal
with drum
raise trees kiss earth
open pens break doors use
stones and blades arrows and fists
fight
free more.
and so and so and so again
moon rise sun sleep
more here here here
free.
go back
free more.
over over
they childrens they childrens they
children carry they story

sharon bridgforth

in cloth
in feet
with hair
when laugh
with drum
Praise memory
Praise the people
drum bend holla dance shout laugh free far away
back a woods yonder
free
free more.

drum bend holla dance shout laugh free far away
back a woods yonder
free
free more

drum bend holla dance shout laugh free far away
back a woods yonder
free
free more
free.

drum bend holla dance shout laugh free far away
back a woods yonder
free
free more
free.

bright green and red/deep purple and orange a twist
of yellow hint of pink/blue
in the pot stir and simmer/smell and smile

bitty fon carry all of Africa on she lips / in her hips
she Indian earth tones smooth with the Black of her

28

skin/the rise of she cheek bones
bitty fon be more beauty than beauty can take.
bitty in the jail house dreaming awake/like she
sometimes do
sit with the dead people
dance a little
always with she two thick braids adorning the front she
body.

na dat first ting be da dancing/always dancing must
praise da Earth for She Mother
turn to moon reach for sun call da wind sing for da
went-befores
smile and open yo heart. we guiding/been
watching/keep light on your path. dat second ting is
love. always must love. in fright in sorrow in not
know in leaving always love. nothing else be real/but
love. dat what open da door for da Spirit rest and
touch and move and show and lead your life with
Grace. third ting
be passing it down child to child to child one to da
other
shake gourd free heart move body smudge sing pray
dance drum cry praise laugh smudge sing pray dance
drum cry praise laugh
smudge sing pray dance drum cry praise laugh
for ever and ever
sho nuff   free.

sharon bridgforth

you shoulda loved me better
baby/you know you shoulda loved me right
say/you shoulda loved me better

baby/you know you shoulda loved me right

but you didn't and now you know
you got to get outta here or fight.

the scent of you is still on my mind/from the last time
you pressed your body against mine.
that was a long time ago.
i know that distance and time
have placed themselves between us
and that my actions from the past remain soured in
your memory
but i am wondering
if you would come close to me   just once more.

the thought of holding you
fills me now
and desire has made me dizzy/with the urgency of
knowing how things
could be.
please
let me hold you   come here.
baby?

lil tiny working on getting back in the house   again.
she done got throwed out
tossed back/throwed out/kept in/throwed out/put on
a pallet
all by she self/many times since the day of she
mess-up/following lushy's fool ass.

ruthieann soonyay got lil tiny living on
training ground.
na/i
ain't finding nothing wrong with that.
break them down i say/break them down.

lil tiny gone have to work real hard
for a let in/stay in.
and even when lil tiny do get let in for a stay in/it ain't
gone
never
be like it was before   cause na
ruthieann looking at lil tiny through a scar in she
memory/ain't gone be easy to open all the way again.
wellsuh/these things are just all part of it.

see/love
feel easy at first.
when you ain't working on nothing but keeping a face
full of one the other/love
feel easy.
but when you decide
you want to stay in love
you gots to work.
you gots to look at love
rumble with it
choose it
and give all of yourself to it/everyday   if you wants to
stay
in a good love that is.

> them ones what looking like they always saying
> the right thing/smiling/never
> misunderstanding/not crying/no acting
> out/seem all happy/huggy/sweety sweety/this

31

>> and that   they is lying!

i know this
cause i done had relations with half the lying loves
around here.
not that they was lying to me
naw
i the one they lying about.

see/i just show up
get what i come for/move on.
>> swing in
>> swing out/gone.

>>> thats why they calls me cat.
>>> yessuh/my kitty is full grown and well known
>>> you see. she bite you hold you fit you lick
>>> you/and spit you out.
>>> done made the hardest of the hard fall
>>> crazy/broken
>>> and spent. done had the best of
>>> mens/wy'mns/and the neithers.

>>> kitty
>>> done left my name/tip of many a tongue/till
>>> now   just a shift of her will do.

yessuh/they calls me
cat
but i'm just a regular kitten/growed powerful.

anyway.
you gots to go through some things if you want a good
love.
which is why folks in love just seem to show out from

32

time to time. oh yeah
and lil tiny
have showed out with the best of them this time.
so/for now
look like all she gone know of the kitty is ruthieann
swinging in swinging out/gone.
cause ruthieann keeping lil tiny on the training ground.

wellsuh/sometime
it do have to happen like that.
but
the thing
i am wanting to know today is
why is it
that it have always got to be proved
that fat meat is greasy.

the question come to me when i saw
lil tiny
big bill
mannish mary
guitar sam
and lushy
sitting around
smoking cigars and talking low/back of bettyes late on
fried chicken friday.

big bill counsel lil tiny/say
problem is
you talks too much.

and you keeps your thoughts just all on your face.
be getting the i'm sorry/i don't understand/i done messed
up/and i want you look
all over/clear as day.

the wy'mns   they enjoys working on you/just a bit.
it makes them turn/if you show too much of how
ready you are.

you see all them foxes/pulling on me every night.

they comes to me.
i just sits there   encourage they to feel free/to work on me.
if they wants to sit with big bill/they come sits
if they wants to hold on to big bill's arms/they grab the arm
if they wants to sit on big bill's lap/they know they can take
to it/if they want a little kiss/i say gonn on honey have
yourself a kiss   but the kissing/and all that there
ain't really the point
lushy break in say
like hell it ain't the point
of course it's the point/it's the whole gotdamn point
mannish mary grumble
that is exactly why you ain't got no wo'mn
lushy get loud then/say
you ain't got room to be talking about somebody not
having a wo'mn/when you ain't had the nerve to say
more than boo to the only wo'mn that you have ever
loved your entire life.
that catch mannish mary off guard/all she get out is
wellwellwell
lushy say
well well/my ass
you know thats truth.
guitar sam laughing like he watching jackie mably.

big bill go back to it
thing is you gots to give a wo'mn time to show you
what she want   where she at/what she feel like.

thats the point.
you can't be rushing up on her/crowding and strutting
begging and parading your feelings all in her face.

lushy say
shit you know you ain't got to worry about that/lil tiny
too scary to be rushing up on a wo'mn.
mannish mary and guitar sam agree
indeed. and *ain't that the truth*
big bill say
you right/you right on that.
but the main thing is just
don't let the wy'mns know you a fool.
and keep your composition at all times.
lil tiny eyes get big / ask
what you mean composition?

big bill lean up in she chair / look lil tiny in the eye
quiet / then say
well/it's like this here
the wy'mns
they wants to know
that you can
handle
things
and the proof of that
show in how you carry yourself.
so
if you likes a wo'mn
hold back just a bit   give her time to signal you.
if your nerves gets undone in the meanwhile
just lean back/keep a hold of your face/and don't
say nothing
        cause anything you about to say at that point
        probably

ain't gonn be too smart.

take your time   handle yourself
play the situation like a slow drag.
composition. thats what i'm talking about.

lushy put her cigar out / say
bill
i ain't never seen you handle a thing when it come to
bettye.
she got you soft as a gotdamn angel cake.
got you working for free
you cleaning she kitchen back there before
opening/just tonight and
i seen you the one been going sit by her.
she ain't never once walked over to your bench in the
entire gotdamn history of your time up in here.
big bill say
umph. well/that may be the case
but at least i didn't break her heart to shreds/bend it so bad
she can't hardly stand up to love no more/and
mannish mary interupt
wellwellwell
lushy go on/like she ain't even heard big bill outbursts
lil tiny as you can see
ain't none of us really got it all figured out/however
you ain't got no excuse.
big bill still riled
you damn right/she ain't got no excuse   for following
your fool ass through troubles gate!
lushy take offense
focus gotdamnit
you know i didn't have to twist her arm or force her to
show her fool ass ways
big bill say

36

well/you right you right about that
mannish mary nodd
guitar sam raise his drink in toast to it
lushy breathe
guitar sam speak up/he say
lil tiny
i'm thinking
you must like feeling alone and hurt
big bill mannish mary and lushy nodd/agree on this
let guitar sam finish
and that's alright/if that is what you like.
but know this   as long
as you keep on courting pain and misery
thats what you gone find yourself living with.
at that lil tiny just drop she head to the table
and cry.
i stop acting like i'm just happen to be dancing/just go
on sit at the table
join big bill mannish mary lushy and guitar sam in a
moment of silence.

which don't last long/cause we all sick of lil tiny's
showing her ass ways.
so/we get on up and into the business of fried chicken
friday at bettye's.
leave lil tiny at the table with her pain and misery.

take me
take me baby
take me
take me baby
take me
take me baby
take me

37

duckie smooth was a handsome man.
voice river deep/smile mountain wide/eyes shiny
soft/body rippling hard   and/duckie
smooth
was as wonderful to listen to/as to behold.
man always knew just what to say/how to who when
and in what timbre.

that is why bettye felt fine leaving duckie smooth
in charge on buffet night every week
cause bettye knew
that man could talk the hiss out a snake/coax sly out
the fox.
yessuh
duckie smooth in charge every week/on buffet night
over to bettye's.
so bettye always take that night off/it's the one night
she ain't got to cook/cause
ain't no food on buffet night   though anything else
you liable to want
do be served.

na/duckie smooth mama name he john harrison lee.
but we been calling him duckie smooth since that
legendary night john lost his cool/at the second ever
buffet night/long time ago.
i was there.
in fact/i was the one name he
it just come holla out my mouth.

see
duckie smooth
do female interpretations

on buffet night.
na/as handsome a man as john is/it is surprising
at just how ugly a woman he becomes.
but he so classy/he transform from a eyesore to a
beautiful and most desirable human being right before
your eyes
till/the mens the womens the both and the neither
be batting eyes at himshe.

duckie smooth and his wife cora davis
sews all through the days
so that every buffet night
duckie smooth got a fresh getup
for each introducement of the evenings headliners.
duckie smooth fall out fancy shiny sparkly cool seven
eight nine times a buffet night
face caked/different wigs flipping in different directions
for different outfits
and cora davis/always in color coordination going
round and round
collecting appreciation fees from everybody in the joint
yessuh everytime duckie smooth swing out
cora davis right there justa collecting.

anyway
like i said
the night duckie smooth got named
was back on himshe second time doing buffet night at
bettye's.
himshe come out once
come out twice
come out three times
delightful stunning with magnagamous eleganance and
introducements for the peoples.
we was all settled in for a long good time/ready to ball.

39

till
it did seem
we was waiting a bit too long for the fourth interpretive
introducement of the fourth act.
when all of a sudden
we hears

MAFUCKA!

then
bambambam!
out roll onto the stage
john and fathead sims
and before we know'd it fathead had
done yanked the bottom half of john's dress clean off
which really piss john off/so at that point himshe sho
nuff
commenced to kicking fathead's ass
said
i
will
bust
a
new
hole
in
your
ass.
bas
tard!
john just a whooping fathead's ass   till it was over.
john then stand up/all 6 foot of himshe
wig off/face cake caked/titties crooked/and
himshe panties showing just as pink as you please
cause there weren't no dress to cover the bottom half

thats when i find myself yelling
he duck it smooth
he duck it smooth
see john
had done
ducked him manhood so smooth back you
couldn't see not a trace of it
      and i knew how much a tucking that take
      cause / well
anyway
i just knew
so
yessuh
that is how duckie smooth got named
on that famous night himshe loose himshe cool
at the second ever buffet night at bettye's
long time ago.

bring your burdens
               bring your burdens
      bring your fears
               bring your fears
      bring your sorrow
               bring your tears
      lay them down
               down on me
      lay them down
               down on me
      oh down
               down on me
      oh down
               down on me
      oh down

41

> *down on me*
> *oh down*
> *down on me*
> *say lay your burdens*
> *say lay your burdens*
> *down on me*
> *down on me*

sometime
a whole lot of shit just liable to happen.

thats exactly what went through my mind when i saw
j.b. walk up in bettye's that night.
bitty in jail nigga red shot down big mama sway so
damn fine she like to kill us all
lil tiny crying/big bill up to something/who know what
and then
in walk j.b.

now
j.b. mama name she lucinda davis/but we been calling
her j.b.
          short for juicy butt.
all the davis girls gots some prosperous behinds
but i declare/j.b.   the most richly endowed.
it got to do with the way she walk/roll it
just so
like she a queen/moving on rose petals and red carpet
like she got a thousand servants trailing back to bid her
due. yep
j.b. very expressive in her exhibition and such.
except some days look like the only trail back of her be
trouble and tears.
like this night when j.b. come up in bettye's.

42

j.b. had decided she want some kokomo bechett this
night
and when j.b. decide she want you/you might as well
just go on and lay down
cause you gonn be got.
problem is
j.b. already have had
and quit
kokomo. after seven years of shacking up
j.b. one day decide she done with kokomo and his old
man ways.
see/kokomo a young man set in settling in. he big
beautiful quiet and sweet. the kind of man that like to
work hard and play hard/but at home. don't need no
streets. j.b. however is fine fast raucous and hot. got to
get out to cool off from time to time.   love don't settle
she down it rile her up. j.b. tried to play at
home/kokomo tried to run the streets but all that
served was to make them twisted.
then one day j.b. got it in her head that all the bending
and changing and settling wasn't right. so
she called it quits.
took the bed the table the chairs the pots the iron the
good dog the rose bush and
her juicy butt/and moved into a cute little old house
yonder.
by herself.
yep
kokomo didn't have nothing but a echo when j.b. got
done.

oooohhweeee
use to hurt our hearts to see poor kokomo after that. it
was like he just flew away/left his body behind. he go

43

to the fish fry the church to bettye's my house your
house everywhere
just sit. no words no smile no breath just stare
off/propped up wherever he was
till the gathering end or somebody take him walk him
on home.
then one day he just disappear into that empty house.
stop coming around.
leaves change
freeze come
spring pass
heat hit
then
there he is
kokomo bechett beautiful as he ever been
eyes bright smile light groomed
and grinding up on her and her and her.
made many a soul grateful to catch sight of kokomo
back in himself.
we see he done filled his house with tables chairs a bed
he made/flowers he planted and tended vegetables he
watered growed.
kokomo had done found and loved his own self/back
to life again.

thats when j.b. decide
she got to have kokomo back.
we telling her to please leave that man alone
j.b. say she be damn if she gonn just sit around/let her
husband have a mafuckn girlfriend.
yep.
so when j.b. step in that night
and kokomo all curly cue in the corner with her and her
and her
i says to myself

sometime
a whole lot of shit just liable to happen.

j.b. swing she stroll over
slow
smiling
pick off her with a quick push of she chair and
her with a powerful back/slap of she hand
and her with a raise of she eyebrow.
roll up on kokomo/before he could jump back
had she breath in him ear she hands in his hand and
that ass on him lap.
yep
he wasn't no more good after that.
it was
over.

oooohhweee/we feared for that man.
all the hearts in the room just drop and scream
naw!
lushy the only one say it out loud though
cause she just don't give a rat's ass
lushy say
look here you gotdamn circle fuckas
ya'll best stay together this time/cause we ain't going
through another break apart like last time.
lushy rocking in she chair say
man was halfway to Jesus time you finished with him
lushy mumble
bet not drag your broke down ass around here this
time/after that woman done finished flogging your
mind with she titties.
we all just shake our heads cause we know
this a time when
a whole lot of shit just liable to happen.

45

j.b. and kokomo don't mind us
they back in love/just that quick
like ain't nothing happened before.

never alone
never alone/you are
never alone

na/dat firs ting be da saddness
always be da saddness jes below da top of
tings.
da saddness   you see
liv'n in da memory you don't know you have
yet

you must go right to it
get under it/stay there

that way the saddness can't catch you not knowing
that way the saddness can't knock you down

second ting be da knowing.
you gots ta know what you know and know
dat you know it
take heed
understand!
where you stand we stand/what you feel we know
as you cry we holla.

big paw uncle daddy and ma dear always talk in
threes
but i can't recall what the third ting of this ting is right
now.

they'll be back/tell it again
and
again.

i left big paw uncle daddy and ma dear's house a long
time ago/went where i was before
but still find myself standing with them   see this
that and they
all day and long into the night
dreaming.
like today   we in the ocean.
waves tall continuous crashing and far as you can see
deep under
sea shells and coral seaweed and moonlight
rise in the night
with a thousand voices talking in melody.
we/in the center carried
pushed in the pull
rocked
gently.

it's not our home but is a place we live
the ocean
big paw uncle daddy ma dear/and me.
my mama too. she there/mostly
quiet
smiling
hold my hand.
chuckle chuckle laugh
big paw uncle daddy and ma dear
laugh too/big ole toothless chuckle chuckle.

we come in she dreams.
tickle
hug tight
stand smile Watch Pray Touch Heal

47

sharon bridgforth

whisper worries away   whisper grief away   whisper loneliness away   whisper fears away
whisper saddness away
with sweetgrass sea salt and sage
copal cedar and moonlight/bring Gifts
joy/here
dreams/here
tenderness/here
Blessings/here
Divinity/here
You/here
Spirit/here
family/here
all here
Lift now
Fly now
Free now
Be now
it's okay
not alone
not alone
not alone
not alone
always/We
whisper
Love.

ga gagaga ga gagaga ga
gagaga gagaga ga
bababa
ga   gagag ga
gagag ga
gagaga bababa

ga gagaga ga gagaga ga
gagaga gagaga ga

48

bababa
ga   gagag ga
gagag ga
gagaga bababa

ga gagaga ga gagaga ga
gagaga gagaga ga
bababa
ga   gagag ga
gagag ga
gagaga bababa

ga gagaga ga gagaga ga
gagaga gagaga ga
bababa
ga   gagag ga
gagag ga
gagaga bababa

gagaga gagaga ga
gagaga gagaga ga
gagaga gagaga ga!

gagaga gagaga ga
gagaga gagaga ga
gagaga gagaga ga!

gagaga gagaga ga
gagaga gagaga ga
gagaga gagaga ga!

gagaga gagaga ga
gagaga gagaga ga
gagaga gagaga ga!

they took his drum.
he make another.
they took his drum
he make another/cut and carve and stretch and lace a
little late late till it new
then drum.
you could hear it cross town and town
which scare ole marsa who send they to take that
drum and that one then beat him and take drum and
beat him and take drum and
beat him.
still/he make another and another
then drum.
then ole marsa send they to take he thumb   toss in
jar
like for pickling.
still he drum
like he daddy he grand and grand and grand before
now/before crossing
he still drum so marsa send they take other thumb he
still drum they take he finger he finger he finger every
time still drum
till none left.
they seal jar place on kitchen table where many have
to pass
remember   stay in place.

then all wee hours he sit and rocking back and forth
cry soft close eyes rocking and rocking till some full
moons pass/one night
he run to dirt trail between back of the big house and
field
jump center
with feet

ba ba ba
make sound
ba ba ba
with him mouth
make sound
gagaga gagaga ga
low to the ground legs bend feet ba ba ba
he spin
gagaga gagaga ga
fast fast stir dirt make dust
ba ba ba
loud and loud
ga gagaga ga gagaga ga
ba ba ba
overseer come but can't get close
dust and wind raise hit face
ga gagaga ga gagaga ga
gagaga gagaga ga
bababa
ga
gagag ga
gagag ga
gagaga bababa
ole marsa run scared
ga gagaga ga gagaga ga
gagaga gagaga ga
bababa
ga
gagag ga
gagag ga
gagaga bababa
ole marsa with gun and whip and more overseers
run through house run in kitchen trying to run out the
back door to stop that drum
ga gagaga ga gagaga ga
gagaga gagaga ga

51

bababa
ga
gagag ga
gagag ga
gagaga bababa
but can't get out the door/in kitchen by table ole marsa
he gun and whip and more overseers stuck   legs
won't move past the table/holding the jar
very still no smile
isadora the conjuration woman/head unwrapped let
thick gray braids stand round face and black eyes on
black black skin she stand there hold jar no smile
let ole marsa can't move not even curse can't raise fist
whip gun or overseers can't beat can't drop his draws
and act the animal he has been can't make no tie and
cut and burn and starve and sell and kill like usual
isadora stand there watch ole marsa eyes get big when
he notice she holding that jar which is empty. she
move her eyes to the table where his scraps from
lunch still scraps and him eyes get big at the plate now
empty cause he know they done fed him them fingers.
him eyes roll back in head
ga gagaga ga gagaga ga
gagaga gagaga ga
bababa
drummer feet too fast to see dust whirl raise the wind
wind knock kitchen door open lift ole marsa up high
in the air drop him down flat on the floor
overseers been knocked down
ga gagaga ga gagaga ga
gagaga gagaga ga
bababa
wind lift marsa high up drop him down
isadora still
watch

52

John Harrison
Shriff Twater

lift bam lift bam
gagaga gagaga gagaga ga
ba ba ba
gagaga gagaga gagaga ga
ten times this go on ole marsa been pass out overseers
too. till
ole marsa's spirit float around the room slam down
into his body on the ground
then ole marsa open his eyes he ain't ole marsa no
more he just john harrison
overseers dead dead dead. isadora say they gone
come back slaves next time.
we leave.
every one of us we leave that night. john don't say a
thing.
we just walk off
ain't no plantation no more never since that time/not
on these grounds.
us
we come here.
this been our home
free
for a long time now.

* * *

one day sheriff townswater just up and freed bitty. he
announce *there is the law and there is the Colored law   in*
this case the Colored law is most appropriate to apply to
bitty's situation. and he is right/after all every Colored
in our county would be locked up if sheriff townswater
only considered *the law* around here. as far as *the law*
was concerned Colored folk didn't have the right to be
alive let alone to move around freely and proud in the
world.

53

anyway
before he made his announcement sheriff townswater
had went over to the next county to discuss the
situation with sheriff townswater senior. they decided
that not only should bitty go free/but she shouldn't
have never been locked up in the first place. na/see
sheriff townswater just happen to be sheriff townswater
senior's favorite son/so truth is he could do anything
he want with no consultation but sheriff townswater do
respect his daddy's opinion so he check in from time to
time on big situations like this and such. this is a
situation in itself when you understand that sheriff
townswater senior is sheriff townswater's daddy on the
White side/which mean sheriff townswater senior is a
White man and sheriff townswater ain't. sheriff
townswater senior/his daddy and his daddy
was sheriffs before he/and they got generations of
townswater sheriffs in many counties around here.
yessuh/the townswaters damn near run this entire state
cause they was the biggest land thieving slave having
Indian killing money hoarding crackers in the history of
these parts.
however/when sheriff townswater senior was a young
man he fell in love with marvis jackson/and lost his
mind. he gave up everything/including
his right to access his cracker inheritance. he moved
over into marvis little two room shack and gave they
only child his last name   which if his daddy wasn't
controlling the klan they would have murdered the
whole house of them first day of the union.
well marvis and sheriff townswater senior-who wasn't
sheriff at the time/was just as happy as happy could
be/till ole man townswater heard his White son
was making nigga babies/he came cross the tracks
quick determined

54

to reclaim his cracker son. and all sheriff townswater
senior's daddy had to do to return him to crackerdom
was threaten to round up every Colored man woman
and child/including marvis and her sweet baby
boy/and burn everybody and all they belongings to the
ground.
well even the crackers know what had happened to
baby Moses' people.
so sheriff townswater senior went on home with his
daddy.
eventually marvis married sooky lewis who is the
daddy of sooky lewis jr. and honré and pauline/and yes
he did father sherriff townswater even to this day.
but sheriff townswater and sheriff townswater senior
have always stayed close.
find any ole excuse to sit with one the other.
anyway

sheriff townswater come back and not only let bitty
out/but put on a jailhouse party so big it took up the
whole jailhouse street   in celebration of bitty's
freedom.
sherriff townswater senior was there. sitting still
looking longing at ole marvis when he think she not
looking.
anyway

and oh you can imagine what seductresses miss peachy
and miss bitty was looking like that day/all dressed in
they finest of finery. chile/i can't even speak it/it race
my heart so.

bitty still return to she ole jail cell from time to time
she say things come to her in there.
i don't know if she know/but i know cause i been living

big mamma sway — Isadora Africa Jr.

long enough to know it
that that Colored jailhouse
is built on unmarked Colored graves.
yessuh.

sheriff townswater let bitty do what she want cause he
understand they is powers greater than the gun and the
badge and the jailhouse.
yessuh
they is.

* * *

big mama sway real name is isadora Africa jr.
they been name her
she mama her mama and her mama after that first
African conjuration woman / whose real name they
don't know   or won't say. everybody call this one
big mama sway cause well   you know
plus nobody dare speak she birth name / call all them
generations of power down. but we ain't crazy / we
know who she is.
hell all you have to do is feel her sing. it's enough to
drive you to rip your heart out
lay it at her feet in offering.
thats in the wee hours of moonlight.

sunshine to sunset / she be in her garden pulling weeds
talking to her flowers and herbs singing quite the
different song with fingers and hips and feet in the
earth.
na / i calls her baybay
cause she my baby brother's second wife sister
chile / who i promised i would always look after the
children   and though they all grown / they still my

baybays.
my name is cat but this one calls me aunty.

i comes by baybay's/bring ole slim
toss him on the hammock under the peach trees   let
him nap whiles i sit on the porch drink them potions
baybay serve to keep my bones strong
         which i do think also keep my kitty purring/and
         tight.
anyway
poor slim don't know but he be drinking potion too.
thats why he always sleep so good through the whole
visit   wake so sweet
and virile.
anyway
after dinner baybay wrap her head
hang she sign out/let folk know the conjuration wo'mn
is ready.
but in the sunrise
she ain't nothing but my lil baybay
playing in she garden
talking to the babies to come.

i talk to them too from time to time.
especially this one little ole gal
she real sweet. remind me of baybay/except that one
drawn to heartbreak.
see her conjuration gonn be so powerful/it's gonn tip
her
till she figure out how to adjust her impulses.
yessuh/that one gonn be a isadora Africa jr.   a city
gurl/too far
from home.

she ain't coming for a long time. baybay

gone guide her the whole way.
and me too.
we working with her now.
listen

there go baybay singing with the trees
planting all that needs be known
deep and in the breeze.

* * *

they surround the grounds
sit and stand quiet and still.
feathers tall/faces painted/buck skins/and pipes/come round on
horse and foot
Black black and Indian red and Black Red lifting White white
bodies
fly away   praying and thats not all...
that's nigga red
talking to peachy soonyay.
peachy got no tolerance for nothing red got to say/say
what you telling me this for? i ain't your priest this
ain't no gotdamn confessional and that ain't the blood
of Christ you drinking
thats one hundred and ten percent full fledged stump
liquor/you done snuck up in bettye's. you better hope
she don't pass by/smell you all liquored up like you is
up in here   shiiit
bettye liable to cut your throat with no goodbye. hell
i'm liable to do it my damn self.
nigga red
          who we now calls just red cause she trying so
          hard to give up her nigga ways
keep on pushing/say
we are the ones they tossed overboard. we been already dead.

58

came back get them go.
stand as witness/then walk away with them. cross the fields
the woods the swamp the river   never look back.

i keep having this dream
this same dream ova and ova till it na so loud so many times i
ain't even got to be sleep to see it   this same dream
feathers tall/painted faces/buck skins/and pipes
they sit on horses some stand in a circle one dance like a drum
ga ga ga round and round he go so fast ga ga ga round and round
his feet don't touch the earth. the rest of them fly round/circle
looking at me/pointing trying show me something   only i
can't see it
i can't never see it.
but i see them feathers tall/painted faces/buck skins/and
pipes/they sit on horses some stand in a circle around the circle
they fly away with them white bodies/Praying.

i don't know
i don't know/i guess i don't know/i thought you could help me
figure this thing out.
maybe my dreams might stop feeling like nightmares if i could
understand what they trying to show me.

**hell it ain't your dreams you got to worry about/it's
your gotdamn evil ass heart. everybody know that.
peachy trying to control she temper / cause now that she
ain't scared of red
she real angry.
you got so much hate packed up in your heart it's a
wonder it has not exploded.
but then maybe it has. maybe that's what them
dreams is all about/your evil ass heart crying in the
night.
peachy take some time just stare at red. every time red**

go to open her mouth
peachy hold a beautiful long nailed finger up/shush
her.
after while red start to sweating/sneak a swig down
and one two three more.
peachy stare. red sweat. peachy stare. red swig. stare
swig silence.

finally
peachy say
they are trying to show you something alright.
they trying to show you something and you got so
many walls round your Soul you can't see a thing. i
can see some things though/things i wish i could have
seen and made clear long before the first time you
knocked me upside my head.
i can't go back
but i sure as hell can move forward.   and i am
thinking that telling you this here is just what i need to
push on along.
silence.
stare.
swig.

i see that you is mean
you unrepented
and you ruthless.
you thump that bible and rock in church all of sunday
but in your heart you ain't nothing but a evil drunken
fool that need to search out a way to make right all the
wrong you have done/not just me
but so many others before.
red go to say something but peachy put a finger
up/shush her.
you done carried out selfish decisions/you done

misplaced hate upside the head of many a woman
and the truth is
you ain't even sorry/not one bit.
peachy sit back for a minute/then lean up
continue
i do believe that them White bodies you seeing them
Black and Red and BlackRed ones carry off ain't
nothing but your dead kinfolk carrying the slavers
away to be Prayed over cause they didn't want them
souls coming back mean torturous and full of hate
again.
but i bet every now and then
a Soul or two fall from the Grace of Prayers.
yessuh i think that's what happened to you. you ain't
nothing but one of them White slavers come back
Black and you hate yourself so much till all that hate in
your heart done turned you into your worst nightmare
      a nigga.
peachy just stare at red. red too shocked to say a thing.

finally peachy lean up real close to red
stare her deep in the eyes say
i know why you mean like you is/i understand
the things that have happened to you this life.
but it ain't no reason in the world to ever take your
hurt out on others.
you have blamed everybody around you for your
wounds/but the truth is you allowed yourself to grow
selfish controlling ignorant and just as violent as the
people that hurt you.

your kinfolk giving you the chance to make a turn.
they trying to work with you. but you got to choose to
change right now
or stay the ignorant hatefulass fool that you done

become.
peachy lean in closer
i would not have chosen to speak to you again/ever
but i am glad that you put this moment on me/because
i needed to say these things to you to finish my
business with you for good/for ever and ever.
but
i promise you this
right now this moment/i'm telling you
if you don't get out my face/with all this drinking and
feeling sorry for yourself
i am gonn put you out your misery myself.
bitty missed the mark
but you can believe that i won't.
i got a blade in my hair braid/got your name on it.
at that peachy pulled from she braid a long slender
pearl handled knife/which she opened to reveal a razor
sharp edge. she twirled it out in front of
her/gleeful/but quiet.
red nod her head real fast/snot and tears streaming
down she face
peachy take in the sight of it for a minute/then continue
in the name of the love of bitty fon/my wife/my
protectress/my only love
i swear i will slice the life out of you/if you don't get
out my face right now.
peachy take a breath and lean forward/smile just a little
yessuh i would be happy to sit where my bitty sat in
that jail house for the pleasure of cutting you down.
maybe i should have done that the very first time you
beat the skin off my face/instead of trying to
understand your ignorant ass. but i tell you what
i am telling you na
mafucka get out my face
or die.

you can best believe that red was up and out that jernt
quicker than peachy could lean back in she seat.

every since that day of counseltation with peachy
red been changed. oh yeah/and she dreams change too.
now they start with her seeing she ownself running and
ducking dodging and hiding
from peachy.

yessuh i declare
i always have loved me some peachy soonyay.

* * *

one day things took a turn/and everything changed
or maybe things that already was just came into focus.
well
you ever seen'd two people that truly love each
other/two people that truly love each other but done
had so much hurt pass between them that the old hurts
block the old love but the old love keep a growing
anyway/yet they can't make the old love new because
they can't stand to be around one the other and they
can't take being apart
ummhumm
well
everything was as it had become
till change walked in one night.
she was a gray eyed gap tooth thick lipped cookie
brown woman with tight lightbrown curls rumbling all
the way down to a bounce on her behind   which set
amply high stretching her many colored thin materialed
dress/like a piece of rubber drawed tight.
change had enough curves to make for a long trip

63

sharon bridgforth

and when she walked
she carried you around and around and around with
her. so when change
walked into bettye's that night
ummmhumm
we all knew some shit was liable to happen.

change come swinging in/swirling a little dust before
her as she
head straight for lushy/which is hard to do
cause lushy sit quite far back in bettye's/say
the best table in the jernt be the one bettye don't
serve/which would be any table lushy liable to be at
she just always keep it to the back
well
change was moving toward lushy/like it was a natural
thing
till somebody yell out
that's her that's her!
j.b. and kokomo look up/seem to know who change
was
but instead of sending out a welcome
they packed theyselves up/got on out of bettye's
as did about four or five other peoples.
na/i didn't have time to give much thought to the
leaving   cause i got caught up
in change.
people started yelling begging for a song/i was
watching her
take it all in   till all of a sudden
right there in the middle of the jernt that woman
widened she stance throw'd her head all the way
back/dropped down a taste/open she gap tooth big
lipped mouth
and i declare

the sound that came out
shook the entire room.
shit started flying off the walls/glasses was tumbling
from tables and the peoples damn near made a
stampede getting to the dance floor. i ain't never
experienced nothing like it.
that woman unleashed the power of Gabriel with her
voice
swinging high and low and around the room all at the
same time/knocking everything
to a new place.
it took the band quite a few to pick they drool up and
join in.
meantime/change was shaking she hips hard as she
was shaking them walls
mixing everybody's mind up/till the confusion of so
much movement and feeling exploded in the last note of
she song.
then it got quiet.
change turn
get back in route to lushy.
i says to myself poor j.b. and kokomo was fools to leave
before all this got let out.
ummhumm
well
drool got wiped/the band start back normal/coffee go
to being served/flasks get to being opened and the
dance floor got back to its usual dip.

thats when i turned
saw bettye's face
which didn't look friendly at all
oh she was smiling
like a big ole wild cat tracking it's prey.
oh lawd/na

i shout but can't nobody hear me cause right then
bettye let out a yelling as she broke a pop bottle in
half/move
with the jagged edge face out
na/this cause ten things to happened all at the same
time
change turn round pull something from she
titties/crouch and smile
the dippers pause
lushy run up from back the jernt grab bettye rush she
out the front door
big bill run down from front the jernt pull change out
the back door
papa ann holla and faint the band switch songs/pause
then
folk get back to things and whatnot.
except me.
i roll out front see what going on.
there i find bettye and lushy under the
figure's flavors.   the world's finest.
come get a taste.
sign/which we all reads
bettye's jernt/and
there lushy and bettye talking.
lushy say
look here bettye
it's time you let this thing go.
bettye look violent but lushy press on say
i am sorry bettye i know sorry don't make it right/but i
need to say it to you
i owe you that.
lushy take a big breath then quick start
bettye i was wrong in how i treated you
i was wrong for the way i took your love for granted/i
was wrong to think that i could act any ole kind of

way and that it was your job to take it/i was wrong for
the ways i leaned on you but wasn't around when you
needed to lean/i was wrong for all the nights of
making you worry with my drinking/for making you
guess what was on my mind/for blaming you for
everything that went wrong/for not taking the time to
treat you tender/for not holding up my share of
making our life work/for walking out the door yelling
one last time/leaving you our home all that we had
dreamt and built and still needed to do/for all the
ways that i acted a fool i know i was wrong/and i was
sho nuff wrong
for fucking change bettye.
i am sorry honey.
i am sorry.
lushy stood real close look bettye deep in the eye.
just stand there breathing soft saying she sorry real
low/stare
till/all the wind and flame and will and walls fell away.
and the two of them just collapse into one the other's
arms. bettye crying let lushy hold she/lushy crying let
bettye hold she.   i crying in the corner leaning against
the wall over around the other side of the
figure's flavors. the world's finest.
come get a taste.
sign. which we all know is bettye's jernt

yes sir/i saw it.
i saw the dam break i saw the love flow i saw the stars
sparkle i saw the light shift
that night i saw/wasn't nothing the same
all because the dust got stirred/by change.

bettye drop ten years of bitter off/make she youth shine
lushy we now call by she birth name

again/luiscious/she smile and sweet and calm
like she ain't even herself/but more so is
bettye and luiscious done popped the boards off they
old home/been busy making it new
put slim and duckie smooth in charge of bettye's for a
time
big mama sway be singing in a new style of conjure
song

> *i never left you*
> *i been right here*
> *waiting this whole time*
> *wrapped in the memory of*
> *your smile*
> *your eyes*
> *the scent of you*
> *i been dreaming awake/about*
> *sleeping in the soft of*
> *your breasts falling*
> *around my heart*
> *i been walking in the moonlight*
> *wishing for your love*
> *praying God give me one more chance*
> *to love you right.*

i come to take you home bill.
you got to come on home. you been gone long enough
wandering alone/all them places all them women all them
songs.
you keep yourself layed up but you ain't belonged anywhere or
to anyone since you left home. your heart been crying all this
time. you think Praying on that guitar gonn save you but it
can't   cause you are not even able to fully give yourself to the
song.

68

i know all about it/see
i been feeling every bit of it
from home/i have been with you
so i know it's time. you're tired now baby
i am too. so come on na. it's time for you to come back
look your mama in the eyes
and cry.

you ain't the only one that lost your daddy/we all did
and when you left too
well/that just made it worse.
but you can come home.
he can't. you still have time
he don't.
papa b is dead bill.
but your mama ain't.
your brothers and sisters ain't
and i sho ain't.
you may feel like you is
but you ain't dead neither
you just gone.
so pick that guitar up
and come back to yourself
so you can be free.

* * *

they met over a poem
a poem they wrote in the fields   between the digging
of earth/the
laying of tracks/the crossing of lines. between the
pounding of steel/and sun
with battered Spirits/in open spaces
with no silence   they made poetry
one syllable at a time/they

69

conjured theirselves/love

kiss
me
miss
you
wish
i

touch
me
hold
you
now
i
need
your
love

will
you
be
my.

baby

this is how booka chang and joshua davis found each
other. in
blistering sun/working days never ending/backs bent
in toil/in
the company of men   they claimed each other
declared themselves
adorned each other with words. united
in heart/booka chang and joshua davis married one the
other

with a poem.

love
you
live
with
me
love
you
live
with
me

my
man
my
man

for
all
time
for
all
time

i
am
yours
i
am
yours.

they quit the rails. opened shop
selling charms and things right there in they front yard
they give poetry for free.

71

sharon bridgforth

and even us that make our own charms stop by cause
some days/you just need
a poem.

*hold
me
with
your
eyes*

*make
me
know
i'm
yours*

*give
me
all
you
have*

*fill
me
with
your
heart*

dear.

* * *

*we took her to booka chang and joshua davis/for a charm
a chance to know what it feels like to hold hope*

but for some   a charm
ain't easy.   for some/a charm
take Work.

booka look at joshua
joshua look at her
her look away
joshua sing
booka clap
we move   circle
she fall out
in circle
we move left
make remembering
make occurrences
make the Work.

and we seen it as
booka and joshua read it
in a poem
in the circle
clap
us moving left
her falled out
booka and joshua say

sun
river
you

you
river
sit

sun

heat
river

river
move
slow.

river
move
slow.

sun
moon
cross

stars
shine
soft

you
river
gaze

river
move
loud

your
head
spins

river
move
fast

your
heart
jumps

river
change
shape

your
eyes
lock

river
rain
down

river
rain
down

blood
rain
down

fill
river
thick

run

you can't.

wind

sharon bridgforth

cry
names

trees
know
names

wind wail
river thunder
trees moan

you

can't

move.

you
can't
cry
you
can't
breathe
you
can't
see

river
pulls
you
in

rain

keeps
you
under

river
sweeps
you
down

river
carries
you
away

long
journey.

trees
wind
sun
river
you.

home.

yessuh.

we calls her miss sunday morning
but she don't hardly go to church   though she do
rock with sweet t lashay/pray to god
every Sabbath.

miss sunday morning run the jernt
back of bettye's.

it's a gambling shack
a place standing way past good timing/she
gots folks working dark corners back rooms against the
walls
and on a little red lighted stage   be shake
dancers/grind so hard
not a string of clothing can hang on   they bump and
wiggle
into the night and sunrise/dancers drop so far down
squeeze the last note out any song   rolling
back up.
yessuh
miss sunday morning gots a little something for
anybody/just outside of right.
folk stepping in know   all possibilities
gonn come to pass.
they is jimmy slide/he smoke a cigarette with him
asscheeks   suck/tight
whip the mind of many around at the sight of it.
they is sally thick/who move she hips so slow
and low/and deep into the night
till ain't nobody brave enough to do nothing but watch.
her
off in a blue light
on a table
smiling and winking and
riding
alone.
they is tucker long who gots a peter and putter
open and unroll/let you touch
for a fee

and they is them that fill the jernt
so tender/and flush
so ready

and ripe
so full of bursting
ain't nothing but trouble in sight.

yessuh
we gives miss sunday morning plenty room.
hard as life is around here/much as we gots to forget
much as we needs to forgive/filled as we is with
knowing
bad as it feel sometime/folks bound to only can find
jesus
over to miss sunday mornings jernt/some folks
got to jump in the circle that way
through the back door.
late.

miss sunday morning herself
come in that way. her and sweet t
come in from a long road
late
and right on time.

see/sweet t was a man last life
is na woman/feel like a man
solid and sturdy/stern and silent/pressed and polished
sweet t
used to not know why he look like a he
packed like a she
sweet t
used to not understand why things didn't fit/why he
didn't make no sense
sweet t used to want to return him   she body
early sometimes
sweet t used to couldn't wait to come back/a he again.
sweet t used to get tired.

sharon bridgforth

look like
sweet t was the one everything bad happened to
the one that never harmed nobody/but always got beat
since she was a child   folk take they evil out on she.
must have been sweet t was the one that suffered our
transgressions
paid the price
for our collective sins. didn't know why.
sweet t had a hard life.
sweet t had it rough
sweet t got scars all over she body.

a man then
woman now/neither really
skin peel/heart pull apart
sweet t journey been long.
no one to talk to. no one to think about the wrong of it.
no one to kiss the pain. no one
to see her. no one to care why
no one

till miss sunday morning come along.

miss sunday morning come in with the river
miss sunday morning floated down   layed up on a
rock/stretched out
sweet t found she

miss sunday morning had got tired too.

far away
she flew
in her mind
spun open
will

80

running
from nothing
running
from everthing
running
for no reason/running
for lots of reasons/running
because.

she left/her body
left her mind
left/floating
with empty eyes/in silence
she left
swept away
landed in the wrong place/at the right time
miss sunday morning opened her eyes saw
sweet t's face and cried.
said i'm home now. and
they didn't need no words. they saw it all in one the
other's eyes
and knew what they knew.

was sweet t brung miss sunday morning to us
brung herself too. said they needed a charm
a chance to make it
wanted the road to be gentle/to
open a little more kind

and so now miss sunday morning and sweet t
they pray
in each others arms
in each others mouths
bodies wrapped/they make Holy
every Sabbath   love

they blossom
full
raise up one the other/breathe in tongues
take in Spirits/swollow
whole
shine
perfect in the light
of Sabbath
when the jernt is closed
they lay up
in one the other
breasts full
hips open/and large
like sunshine/they move
up and down
side to side across the sky
deep penetrating
and all day/reaching
higher
higher
lift
smile
see
God
cry
wail
sing
see
each other
heat
rise
moan
burst
make

82

love
Holy
Wholy
make
love
every day
and all of
Sabbath.
when the jernt is closed.

sweet t gots a little girl in he/now
giggle giggle slip out here and there/all the time since
miss sunday morning got a hold of she.
sweet t don't understand it/but ain't mad at why.

miss sunday morning and sweet t run that jernt together
na
make provisions for the peoples.
keep the back door open

Holy Wholy everyday
Holy Holy they love
Holy Holy they love
Holy Holy love
Holy
they...

bettye figurman slim figurman luiscious boudreaux cat
lil tiny ruthieann soonyay peachy soonyay bitty fon
king creole red guitar sam mannish mary kokomo j.b.
duckie smooth cora davis fathead sims change big bill
henry b mama stonwell marvis jackson sherriff
townswater booka chang joshua davis reverend honré
sooky lewis sooky lewis jr. pauline miss sunday

sharon bridgforth

morning sweet t lashay big paw uncle daddy ma-dear
the drummer the Houma the Fon the Ibo the Yoruba
the Wolof the Tunica the Choctaw the Chickasaw
isadora Africa jr. isadora Africa jr. isadora Africa jr.
isadora Africa jr. isadora Africa jr. isadora Africa jr.
here with me here in me/are   me...

our gurl she
carry the conjuration her mama she mama she mama she mama
and that first African woman pass on   this scare her from
time to time/cause there are things she know but don't understand
things she can do but don't know why/power she got   can't control
like her voice
it contours time in release
each note/make the Holy Ghost rise in all who feel
she don't question this
but it do make her sad. too much too big too often/alone.
can't wrap words around it/so she don't try. just keep to herself
except for times when she think she drowning
feel like a touch/some talking/a smile might save her.
she keep company then

our gurl
she hurt from feeling all the the feelings she feel
which she keep pushed down/cause she think she got to
can't stop stay sharp turn the check toss the head step on be strong don't worry never want
can't have don't rest
smile
one foot in front the other/heavy
not dreaming
whittle words
day by day
till
nothing left

84

our gurl don't yet understand that the pressure of not feeling/explodes
poisons the Spirit dims the vision stills the heart cripples the hearing sickens the body makes
lonely the path
which liable to make the lesser way seem right at the cross roads
so
we told she mama/to send
our gurl home
na!

i'm gonn bring my burdens
i'm gonn bring my fears
i'm gonn bring my sorrow
i'm gonn bring my tears
i'm gonn lay them down
gonn lay them down
i'm ready/i am
ready to lay my burdens down.

our gurl don't even know how she know that song/but she know it make her feel better
so she sing it all the time. yessuh
we bringing our gurl home   to teach her some things
let her see for sho for sho she not never alone/not ever.
our gurl   she the one

isadora Africa jr
hands in earth
conjuration she.

booka chang joshua davis clap speak   conjuration she
bitty fon/dreaming dream   conjuration she
big mama sway/sing shake   conjuration she
peachy soonyay/claim her power   conjuration she
jook jernt/holla dip   conjuration she
ma-dear big paw uncle daddy/pray smile   conjuration she

85

sharon bridgforth

drummer/drumming drum   conjuration she

                    African and Indian/fly free conjuration
                              she/says our names
                                 conjuration/she
                               keep our stories
                                conjuration we

send she back   conjuration we
hold her hands   conjuration we
praise she laughter   conjuration we
pave her path   conjuration we
open her road   conjuration we
Bless her heart   conjuration we
join her Love   conjuration we
grant she wishes   conjuration we
give her riches   conjuration we
stand in Light   conjuration she
sits in gold   conjuration she
dresses in jewels   conjuration she
says our names

                              conjuration
                                  we
                                 give
                                  she
                                  Life
                              conjuration
                                  we

                                 here
                                 here
                                 here
                              conjuration
                                  we

                                 here
                                 here
                                 here

conjuration
We

She...

You are the me i am waiting to be
deep down/i see your Divinity
and i know that we are Free.
free/like the night in flight
free in God's Delight
in the Name of/We are

flesh of the Ocean
the Sun beaming bright
Winds crossing
the Earth's might
we are/your smile
my Heart
with Sight
Free.

no more fighting
i rebuke all fears
no separation/cause we are

the Peace we Pray
the poem we pen
the bridge we make
the song
that dance/is us
and we are

free

sharon bridgforth

                    free
                    Free.
                cause/We are
                    Love.

i   i
am the conjure.   am the conjure.
sacrificial blood made flesh/i am   sacrificial blood made
sanctified by tears wailing   flesh/i am
deep in the belly/i am that sound   sanctified by tears wailing
released. i am   deep in the belly/i am that
love remembered   sound
the promise kept   released. i am
the should have been   love remembered
the utterance of hope/i am   the promise kept
the Life dreamt   the should have been
                                the utterance of hope/i am
i am the answered Prayer   the Life dreamt
the manifested Light
i am my Ancestors   i am the answered Prayer
returned   the manifested Light
i am the dead/and the living   i am my Ancestors
i will carry on   returned
i will come back   i am the dead/and the
i will grow more powerful   living
i will remember   i will carry on
i am the one We are waiting for i will come back
i   i will grow more powerful
am   i will remember
the conjure   i am the one We are
come back/to Love.   waiting for
                                i
                                am
                                the conjure
                                come back/to Love.

                        88

remember
remember
remember.

About the Author

Sharon Bridgforth is the Lambda Award-winning author of *the bull-jean stories* (RedBone Press), and *love conjure/blues*, a performance/novel published by RedBone Press. The premiere performance of *love conjure/blues* was produced by The University of Texas at Austin's Center for African & African American Studies. Bridgforth is an Alpert Award Nominee in the Arts in Theatre; her work has been presented nationally at venues, including: The Madame Walker Theatre Center—Indianapolis, IN; Walker Art Center—Minneapolis, MN; the Michigan Womyn's Music Festival—Walhalla, MI; and Highways Performance Space—Santa Monica, CA. Bridgforth has received support from the National Endowment for the Arts Commissioning Program; the National Endowment for the Arts/Theatre Communications Group Playwright in Residence Program; and the Rockefeller Foundation Multi-Arts Production Fund Award.

Bridgforth has developed an innovative style of teaching creative writing that she calls *Finding Voice*. Bridgforth has facilitated the *Finding Voice* method as part of long-term residency programming for institutions around the country, including The Austin Project (sponsored by The University of Texas at Austin's Center for African & African American Studies); Hamilton College—Clinton, NY; and the Austin Latina/Latino Lesbian Gay Bisexual Transgender Organization (ALLGO)—Austin, TX. Bridgforth is executive producer of the *Finding Voice Radio Show*, funded by the Funding Exchange/The Paul Robeson Fund for Independent Media.

For more information go to www.sharonbridgforth.com and www.loveconjureblues.com.

Other titles from RedBone Press include:

does your mama know? An Anthology of Black Lesbian Coming Out Stories, ed. by Lisa C. Moore (ISBN 0-9656659-0-9) / $19.95

the bull-jean stories, by Sharon Bridgforth (ISBN 0-9656659-1-7) / $12.00

the bull-jean stories (Audio CD), by Sharon Bridgforth (ISBN 0-9656659-2-5) / $12.99

last rights, by Marvin K. White (ISBN 0-9656659-4-1) / $14.00

nothin' ugly fly, by Marvin K. White (ISBN 0-9656659-5-X) / $14.00

Where the Apple Falls, by Samiya Bashir (ISBN 0-9656659-7-6) / $14.00

Spirited: Affirming the Soul and Black Gay/Lesbian Identity, ed. by G. Winston James and Lisa C. Moore (ISBN 0-9656659-3-3) / $16.95

Blood Beats: Vol. 1 / demos, remixes & extended versions, by Ernest Hardy (ISBN 0-9656659-8-4) / $19.95

Erzulie's Skirt, by Ana-Maurine Lara (ISBN 0-9786251-0-2) / $15.00

Voices Rising: Celebrating 20 Years of Black Lesbian, Gay, Bisexual and Transgender Writing, ed. by G. Winston James and Other Countries (ISBN 0-9786251-3-7) / $25.00

You can buy RedBone Press titles at your local independent bookseller, or order them directly from the publisher (RedBone Press, P.O. Box 15571, Washington, DC 20003). Include $2.50 shipping for the first book and $1.00 for each additional book.